Confusion Is a State of Grace

Confusion Is a State of Grace

Humor and Wisdom for Families in Recovery

written and edited by
Barbara F.

 HAZELDEN®

INFORMATION & EDUCATIONAL SERVICES

Hazelden
Center City, Minnesota 55012-0176

Library of Congress Cataloging-in-Publication Data
F., Barbara
Confusion is a state of grace : humor and wisdom for families in recovery / written
and edited by Barbara F.
p.   cm.
Includes bibliographical references.
ISBN 1-56838-089-5
1. Quotations.   I. Title

PN6080.F48 1995   95-15680 CIP
                                                             082—dc20

Editor's note
Hazelden offers a variety of information on chemical dependency and related
areas. Our publications do not necessarily represent Hazelden's programs, nor do they
officially speak for any Twelve Step organization.

This book is gratefully dedicated to the
Thursday Alamo Al-Anon nonsmoking group.

Contents

Preface

Four years ago I feared there was something dreadfully wrong in my family. My mental health was failing and so was my marriage. As my three babies grew into teenagers, I had to face the painful reality of placing a loved one into a long-term drug program. Everything felt as if it was my fault. Why couldn't my family return to normal?

I heroically put out fires with law enforcement officials; attempted to fix the drug problem by moving to a different town; tried religious help, counseling, marriage counseling, and finally drug treatment. It was the drug counselor who suggested Al-Anon.

Obediently, I attended my first meeting. I expected to be told what to do. I wasn't. I wanted to find the leaders to guide me. There weren't any. I expected to be judged by my appearance, home, career, and reputation. But nobody cared how I looked on the outside. What I did find was people, men and women from all walks of life, honestly opening up about their problems. Some of their problems were even worse than mine—yet these people were enjoying themselves, even laughing!

At the meetings I heard things that made sense. I learned that I kept myself running in circles with my familiar self-talk—*Oh it's not that bad,* or *What did I do wrong?* or *Can't he see what he's doing to me?* It was a relief to hear *Let go and let God, One day at a time,* and *Progress not perfection.* It encouraged me. But would it last when I crossed into the war zone of my home? One day in the midst of a crisis, with doors slamming and insults flying, I ran to my room. Just when I was about to begin crying, "Why me?" I found myself saying the first line of the Serenity Prayer over and over again: "God, grant me the serenity to accept the things I cannot change." Somehow, a small part of me felt safe—and relieved that I didn't have to solve this problem

This was how I started using recovery sayings. I never did get my family back to "normal." But as a friend said, "Normal is just a setting on the dryer." Today I have something much better than normal. I have an appreciation of how unique the people in my family are, including their challenges. With much gratitude for all that has been given to me, I want to share these sayings of hope and wisdom that have been offered by members of the Al-Anon program. You may not agree with all of them, but just *take what you like and leave the rest*. I hope the wisdom of the program will bless your life as it has mine.

Acknowledgments

This book came from hundreds of meetings and hundreds of people willing to share their hurt, their truth, and their triumphs. Thank you!

A special thanks to Bob S. who kept the ball rolling by offering his collected sayings and his time and encouragement to this book.

Also thanks to our anonymous typist who worked many hours giving impeccable form and creative editing to the manuscript.

This would not be complete without recognizing the encouragement and pride I have always felt from my parents, Jeannette and Ken.

And to my husband, Jaime; my children, Miguel, Maya, and Maggie; and my stepchildren, Lena and Tracy; I love you and thank you for being in my life and for being an important part of this book.

I also have been gratefully touched by you, the reader. In Al-Anon we know that we hurt the same and laugh the same. We are not alone. This book shows that our love has spilled over into your hands.

Today

When I'm overwhelmed, I do only
what is essential.

Have a nice day unless you've
made other plans.

I have a wonderful life; I just forgot
what it feels like.

Today is the tomorrow I was afraid of.

You have all the time there is;
there isn't any more.

If you want to see God laugh,
show Him your plans.

We can't control the direction of the wind,
but we can adjust our sails.

If you can't be happy with what you have,
how can you be happy with more?

When I take the credit for God's work,
my serenity is in trouble.

Intuition operates in the present tense.

Never look back—it might be
catching up with you.

—Satchel Paige

The universe is full of magical things patiently
waiting for our wits to grow sharper.

—Eden Phillpotts

Life is what happens when you're
too busy to make plans.

Save time for silence in your day.

I read so many self-help books,
I had no self left.

I can't go to Twelve Step meetings
because I'm in sales and I need my ego.

I knew so much more than I understood.

The mind is like a parachute—neither will work unless it's open.

Pray more and make fewer phone calls.

It's not the mountain ahead that wears you out, it's the grain of sand in your shoe.

Real generosity toward the future consists
in giving all to what is present.

—Albert Camus

I want to eliminate human suffering—
namely mine.

My urgency is a sign that I need to
turn things over to God.

I am who I am because of my past,
not in spite of it.

Obsession is a form of fantasy life.

The time you enjoy wasting
is not wasted time.

—Bertrand Russell

There is always enough time to
do what you love doing.

There is a time for every purpose under heaven.

—Ecclesiastes 3:1

Our goal is not to try harder,
but to trust more.

The ability to simplify means to eliminate the
unnecessary so that the necessary may speak.
—Hans Hofmann

The things that are urgent are rarely
important, and the things that are
important are rarely urgent.

Live in the moment.

If it's important it can wait.

It is almost as important to know what is not
serious as to know what is.

—John Kenneth Galbraith

It only takes a slight shift to change *no where*
into *now here*.

Living in the moment means experiencing to
the fullest what nourishes me in the present.

—Dr. Jerry Greenwald

One must grasp the moment with no hands.

Today is a gift; that's why they call it the present.

Say "Good Morning" even if it isn't.

Worry never robs tomorrow of its sorrow;
it only saps today of its strength.
—A. J. Cronin

EGO: **E**dging **G**od **O**ut.

Today I seek to become a little more accepting of myself, a little more comfortable in my own skin.

—Courage to Change

Today, I will act "as if" until it is true.

Don't fret about the coming and going of weeks and months. Each day holds every season within it.

It is harder to see today when we are
looking at tomorrow.

Do not be anxious for tomorrow,
for tomorrow will look after itself.

—Matthew 6:34

Today is a beautiful room that's never
been seen before.

Give up the hope of a better past.

Time and words cannot be recalled.

God is like a great eraser—there is forgiveness
and a new beginning at every moment.

If we trust God with our Eternity, we can
surely trust Him with this one day.

Relationships

What you think of me is none of my business.

A friend is someone who knows all about you
and likes you anyway.

I need to be treated special just to feel normal.

Don't compare your insides to
other people's outsides.

We all know we are unique individuals, but we tend to see others as representatives of groups.

—Deborah Tannen

HALT: Take care of yourself when you get
> **H**ungry,
> **A**ngry,
> **L**onely, or
> **T**ired.

Resentment is when I take the poison
and wait for you to die.

Alcoholics are in full flight from reality,
and we seem to like to chase after them.

Compare—Despair.

The only thing worse than comparing
ourselves to others is criticizing ourselves
for comparing ourselves to others.

Some people will never get ulcers.
They're just carriers.

When I go to Twelve Step meetings, I come in
with a list of people who need to be there too.

Detachment with love means I should stop
depending upon what others do, say, or feel
to determine my own well-being.

If I love you, I won't hurt you. And if
I love you, I won't be your servant.

One person can't cooperate.

Going to some people for love is like going to
the hardware store for bread.

How can I make a love withdrawal if my
partner is emotionally bankrupt.

I'm always trying to give people stuff
before they want it.

There are no victims, just volunteers.

We are the manufacturers of our own misery.

Don't give advice unless it's asked for.

You are not responsible for making other
people's lives work, they are.

Happiness can be felt only if
you don't set conditions.

—Arthur Rubinstein

Expectation is a premeditated resentment.

It's mind over matter. When you no
longer mind, it doesn't matter.

Love your neighbor,
yet pull not down your hedge.
—George Herbert

Trying to control my loved ones
was like trying to milk a mouse.

Don't try to make pigs sing. It's a waste
of time, and it annoys the pigs.
—Mark Twain

I will allow my children to navigate
their own relationships.

The hardest lesson in life next to death
is teenagers.

Love others enough to let them feel their
sadness, anger, and self-pity. God does.

I can take my sails out of their wind.

Hug 'em, dust 'em off, and let 'em go.

Insanity is doing the same thing over and over again expecting different results.

When somebody bugs me, I can say, "Wow, there's a piece of myself that I don't want."

Awareness does not give advice.

If you have nothing to defend,
life becomes easier.

—Sanaya Roman

Arrogance is the flip side of fear.

Give to others what you want to receive.

Don't have a conversation with someone
who is not in the room.

Maturity is the capacity to withstand ego-destroying experiences and not lose one's perspective in the ego-building experiences.
—Robert K. Greenleaf

Revealing my vulnerabilities gives others the opportunity to be human.

If it feels crazy, it probably is.

Let go of the myth that certain relatives care.

It's a lot easier to find my truth when I'm not
trying to prove your lack of it.

Don't let an insane person take your inventory.

Do I want to set a boundary or
do I want to punish?

Setting boundaries isn't a control issue;
it's a self-love issue.

It's hard to make your life fit someone
else's value system.

If you're bent on revenge,
you'd better dig two graves.

Detachment is not caring less,
it's caring more for my own inner peace.
—*In All Our Affairs*

"No" is a complete sentence.

All progress must grow from a seed
of self-appreciation.

—Courage to Change

I am harming myself if I act as though someone else's life is more important than mine.

Do I really know God's will for the person
I'm trying to help?

Use God as a steering wheel, not a spare tire.

Happiness is not a destination;
it's a form of travel.

God, release me from the bondage of worrying
over what people think of me.

A man lies to others so that he may
lie to himself.

—Japanese proverb

All I thought about was me;
all I talked about was me;
all I got was me.

Your shortcomings are easy to see but teach
me little; mine are hard for me to see
but teach me volumes.

Codependent: When everyone else's opinion
counts more than my own.

Conflict

Love doesn't come with threats.

Nothing pays off like restraint of
tongue and pen.

Do unto others as you would have them
do unto you.

—Luke 6:31

God grant me the sense of proportion to judge
the difference between an incident and a crisis.

Look in the mirror
instead of the magnifying glass.

You can't hold a man down
without staying down with him.
—Booker T. Washington

I didn't think I was judgmental;
I thought I was right.

It's really hard to let someone in my family
be angrier than I am.

For me just to stay with the pain, own it,
and not go into blame—now that
is a spiritual awakening.

Before speaking, ask whether it is true,
necessary, or kind.

In nature there are neither rewards nor
punishment; there are consequences.

—R. G. Ingersoll

You don't have to have a reason to say "No."

The person who sits at the bottom of a seesaw marriage has pockets filled with rage.

Answers are not a substitute for feeling safe.

Hurt people hurt people.

In nature things move violently to their place and calmly to their place.

—Francis Bacon

Didn't cause it, can't cure it, can't control it,
but I sure can contribute to the insanity.

There is nothing wrong with wanting to
change someone else. The problem is
that it doesn't work.

Live and let live.

Anger is not getting my way in the present.
Fear is not getting my way in the future.
Resentment is not getting my way in the past.

Separation anxiety is the disturbing sense
of aloneness we feel when we expose
our differences.

Relationships benefit from a lower degree
of emotional reactivity and a higher degree
of self-clarity.

—Harriet Goldhor Lerner

Compassion comes before forgiveness.

But you must remember, Thomas, that
catharsis is not necessarily revelation.

—Gertrude Stein to Thomas Wolfe

Is your motive to teach or to punish?

Criticizing others is like shining a spotlight in
their eyes; then they can't see anything at all.

Whatever you point a finger at will grow.

When judgment gives way to observation,
anxiety becomes contentment.

What we defend against we make real.

Compassion is the ability to put yourself
in the other person's shoes.
—Sanaya Roman

Harsh words come from someone
who is in pain.

When we fight and blame, we stay on a merry-go-round called denial.

I don't have to think that way anymore.

We are as sick as our secrets.

It is hard to fight an enemy who has outposts in your head.

—Sally Kempton

Nothing on earth consumes a man more
completely than the passion of resentment.

—Friedrich Nietzsche

No God—no Peace.
Know God—know Peace.

Anger is one letter short of danger.

When angry, count to ten before you speak;
if very angry, a hundred.

—Thomas Jefferson

God gave us two ears and one mouth,
which means we should listen twice
as much as we speak.

Do you want to be right or happy?

Tell the truth and let go of the outcome.

If your God isn't big enough to take
your anger, get a bigger one.

Lord, when we are wrong, make us willing
to change. And when we are right,
make us easy to live with.

—Peter Marshall

When you are white-water rafting and you're
headed for a rock, don't paddle madly; stop
and let the current guide you around it.

Great Spirit, help me never to judge another
until I have walked in his moccasins.

—Sioux Indian prayer

Insanity is thinking that we have control.

I planned an intervention, but my
husband didn't show up for it.

What is loving to the self is
always loving to others.

The emotional state we're in is never wrong.

Whoever fights monsters should see to it that
in the process he does not become a monster.

—Friedrich Nietzsche

If you don't feel your feelings,
you act them out.

No man can think clearly when his
fists are clenched.

—George Jean Nathan

If one throws salt at thee, thou wilt receive
no harm unless thou hast sore places.

—Latin proverb

Change comes from practicing
something different.

When you can't get close to God,
get close to people.
When you can't get close to people,
get close to God.

You deserve love, care, and someone to listen
to you, especially after a conflict.

Forgiving is not forgetting;
it's letting go of the hurt.

Guilt

Feeling guilt is usually attached to an
"I should . . ."

No one can make you feel inferior
without your consent.

—Eleanor Roosevelt

I'm all about everything or I'm all about nothing.

It's tough being an egomaniac
with an inferiority complex.

It wasn't the outside problems,
it was the inside feelings.

I always felt better than or worse than—
but never equal to.

I was either a dictator or a doormat.

I wasn't just a doormat;
I was wall-to-wall carpeting.

Creativity comes from being tolerant
of making mistakes.

Help them to take failure, not as a measure of
their worth, but as a chance for a new start.

—Book of Common Prayer

Self-confidence is not the same as self-esteem.

It requires a lot of effort to hold myself
above the others.

It is difficult to make a person miserable while
he feels worthy of himself and claims kindred
to the great God who made him.

—Abraham Lincoln

The amount of shame you have
is equal to the rejection you feel.

I'm like the woman who found a man
wearing a ski mask and holding a knife
breaking into her house. When he told
her, "Oh, I'm a banker," she said,
"Then let me make a deposit."

My mother is a travel agent for guilt trips.

God doesn't make junk.

I don't have to love the situation,
but I can love myself in it.

Feel it to heal it.

Guilt: The way you act when you get caught.

Get off the cross; we need the wood.

Doubt is not a character flaw;
it is an opportunity.

Sometimes it is necessary to reteach
a thing its loveliness . . . until it
flowers again from within.
—Galway Kinnell

The mind grows by what it feeds on.
—Josiah G. Holland

At first I had to "act as if"
I believed that I'd be cared for.

Change your thoughts and
you change your world.

—Norman Vincent Peale

Happiness is wanting what you have,
not having what you want.

Pride: The feeling you get when people
believe your bull.

Every good thought you think is contributing
its share to the ultimate result of your life.

—Grenville Kleiser

Everyone is responsible
and no one is to blame.

The purpose of making mistakes is to
prepare myself to make more.

God, give me the courage to let myself fail.

God chooses to do His work
with imperfect instruments.

My attitude is the words I use
to talk to myself.

Experience is not what happens to you, it is
what you do with what happens to you.

—Aldous Huxley

We can't always stop negative thoughts,
but we can send positive thoughts
alongside of them.

Human beings, by changing the inner attitudes of their minds, can change the outer aspects of their lives.

—William James

Peace is life without envy.

Most of the shadows of this life are caused by standing in one's own sunshine.

—Ralph Waldo Emerson

I am learning to treat myself as if I am valuable. I find that when I practice long enough, I begin to believe it.

—In All Our Affairs

I am enough!

We're here to recognize our magnificence and divinity—no matter what they told us.

—Louise Hay

Refuse to live down to anyone's expectations.

If you have "de-fences" around you,
it's because you need "dem."

Think for yourself, and let others enjoy
the privilege of doing so too.

—Voltaire

To love oneself is the beginning
of a lifelong romance.

—Oscar Wilde

Worry is interest on money you never borrowed.

Though no one can go back and make a brand-new start, anyone can start from now and make a brand-new end.

Of all the people you will know in your lifetime, you are the only one you will never leave or lose.

Pain and Fear

The will of God will never place you
where the grace of God can't help you.

Everything has its wonder, even darkness and
silence, and I learn whatever state I may be in
therein to be content.

—Helen Keller

Fear is the darkroom where
negative thoughts are developed.

. . . when we bring things out into the light
they lose their power over us.

—In All Our Affairs

If I don't want to hit bottom,
I have to stop digging a hole.

Religion is for people who are scared of hell,
and spirituality is for people who
have been there.

—Steve, age nineteen

Pain is the touchstone of all spiritual progress.

Fear exists only when you are running from it.

Fear is like Chinese handcuffs that will tighten
their grasp on your fingers if you pull away.
To release, push into them.

What you resist will persist.

Neurosis is the avoidance of experiencing
legitimate pain.
—Carl Jung

Only my mind can produce fear.

There is no such thing as a problem without
a gift for you in its hands.
—Richard Bach

I want to grow in my willingness
to make room for good times.

—Living with Sobriety

Troubles are often the tools by which God
fashions us for better things.

—H. W. Beecher

Repeating a slogan like "Thy will be done"
can stop rising panic.

Be still and know that I am with you.
—English prayer

Avoiding danger is no safer in the long run
than outright exposure. Life is either a
daring adventure or nothing.
—Helen Keller

I'm learning to let fear walk in and share my
room and leave when it is ready.

To dissolve fear, look directly at it.
—Sanaya Roman

I tried everything to get rid of fear
except not trying to get rid of it.

A way out of a painful situation is to
recognize the part we play in it.

Feelings are emotional energy;
they are not personality traits.

I know a great many troubles.
Most of them never happened.
—Mark Twain

To cope with strong emotions
get the body moving.
—*From Survival to Recovery*

Every fear deserves to be listened to.

Feeling loved changes negative energy.

Talking about my faults gives others
permission to be human.

Say, "I trust that you will make the right
decision for yourself," even when you don't.

Today I'm giving my hurt the same respect
to be here as my happiness.

Before sunlight can shine through a window,
the blinds must be raised.

—American proverb

Don't wait for your ship to come in.
Swim out to it.

A flower has to go through a lot of dirt
before it can bloom.

We are spiritual beings
having a human experience.

Fake it till you make it.

Act as if it were impossible to fail.
—Dorthea Bronde

Expect a miracle.

Life is 10 percent of how you make it and
90 percent of how you take it.

FEAR: **F**alse **E**vidence **A**ppearing **R**eal.

Courage doesn't exist without
encountering fear.

The Chinese word for *crisis* is written with
two brush strokes. The first is for danger and
the second for opportunity.

We walk through darkness to find light,
and walk through fear to find peace.

I crossed a threshold when fear was
my partner not my boss.

The more you understand what you are
learning from a situation, the more rapidly
you can leave it.

—Sanaya Roman

Faith is fear that has said its prayers.

No prayer is wrong to God.

Divine grace is always operating, but in a
crisis the degree of divine intervention
is much greater.

—Mother Meera

Live one moment at a time.

This, too, shall pass.

Death is God's way of saying,
"Your table is ready."

—Barbara Johnson

When I learn to love myself as my Higher
Power loves me, then I'm doing God's will.

Look behind anger to find fear.

Identify the feeling before it has a chance to identify itself as a problem.

Fear is the place where we can practice trust.

I am powerless, but not helpless.

Most people have power steering; we have powerless steering.

Try less and give more.

We cannot climb up a rope that is attached
only to our own belt.

—William Ernest Hocking

There are Twelve Steps on the bridge
that takes me over my pain.

Confusion

Self can't overcome self;
only God can overcome self.

That the birds of worry and care fly
above your head, this you cannot change.
But that they build a nest in your hair,
this you can prevent.

—Chinese proverb

I couldn't find a philosophy of life that would
last for twenty-four hours.

I know I'm having a bad day
when my mind keeps arguing with myself,
and I don't know which side to take.

My head would destroy me if it didn't need
me for transportation.

The human mind always makes progress,
but it is progress in spirals.

—Madame de Stael

Confusion means you're released from the responsibility of knowing the solution.

Life can only be understood backward, but it must be lived forward.

—Soren Kierkegaard

If you work on your mind with your mind, how can you avoid an immense confusion?

—Seng-ts'an

Going in the mental circles of "Who? Why? and How?" keeps us in the problem.

It's frightening being who we really are, but what the hell, somebody has to do it.

We're lost, but we're making good time.

To find out where you're supposed to be, look at your feet.

Common sense will thus become
uncommon sense.

—The Big Book of AA

I identify with the guy who went to *Amnesiacs
Anonymous* and said, "I don't know what
my name is or what my problems are,
but I'm here."

Confusion is a state of Grace.

God is doing for you what you cannot
do for yourself.

Drinking comes before sobriety,
and crisis comes before serenity.

Don't look where you fell;
look where you slipped.

God spare me from what I think
I need to know.

Sometimes the person who makes me feel the most safe also makes me feel the most unsafe.

No one can know in advance all the consequences of making a decision.

I will trust that the answer is inside me and when the time is right, it will become clear.

I find the great thing in this world is not
so much where we stand as in what direction
we are moving.

—Oliver Wendell Holmes

Past failures are guideposts for future successes.

There lives more faith in honest doubt,
believe me, than in half the creeds.

—Alfred, Lord Tennyson

Confusion can be a reminder to look upward.

Nothing changes until it becomes what it is.
—John Bradshaw

We can't move forward until we accept
where we are.

I'm learning to be comfortable with silence
and patient with my presence.

I'm on the other side of something,
but I don't know what it is yet.

Acceptance is mandatory;
understanding is optional.

Chance favors the prepared mind.
—Louis Pasteur

NUTS: **N**ot **U**sing **T**he **S**teps.

A miracle is something so impossible that
unless God is in it, it is doomed to fail.

Starting means you are half done.

It does not matter how slowly you go
so long as you do not stop.

—Confucius

Doubt is your friend asking you to check your
path and providing hurdles to strengthen you.

Don't believe everything you think.

The mind is a valuable enemy.

I feel uncomfortable being silent with most people—and I'm one of them.

I've gotten my mind down to four voices. Now we're a barbershop quartet.

It is an act of courage to acknowledge our own
uncertainty and sit with it awhile.

—Harriet Goldhor Lerner

The solution is here; you just haven't seen it yet.

We are here to learn to see in the dark.

I ask God not for the grace to see
what lies ahead, but for the grace to
accept whatever comes.

—Thomas Merton

etting Go

Do not feel responsible for everybody's happiness.

The people who drive me crazy are reflections of the parts of myself I don't like.

Pray for your enemies even if you start out, "Lord, give that so-and-so what he deserves."

It's hard to shut off the picture of a problem in our mind. We can, however, change the channel.

Prayer is the place where burdens
change shoulders.

God can only fill an empty vessel.

I had to step from the bridge of reason
to the shore of faith.

When you do everything for your kids, you've
given them nothing to do for themselves.

The help I needed was that
I didn't need to help.

Detachment needs to take the form of discreet
friendly silence, not reproachful sulking.

I can give those I love the right
to make their own mistakes.

When in doubt, don't.

I learned to detach in three stages:
First I detached with hate.
Then I detached with indifference.
Now I can detach with love.

Prayer: What you do
when nothing else seems to work.

When we surrender our plans,
miracles happen.

Don't bother to give God instructions,
just report for duty.

When I give the decision away to God,
I am at peace.

Detachment: A bond of mutual respect
for one another's individuality.

If love is in your heart, neither hate, fear,
nor resentment can occupy that spot.

God dwells wherever we let Him in.

One of the hallmarks of emotional maturity is
to recognize the validity of multiple realities.
—Harriet Goldhor Lerner

Make someone's day.
Mind your own business.

If we can find some sunshine while standing
in the rain, we'll make a rainbow.

Opportunity can be disguised as loss.

Welcome loss,
because it opens up the space for gain.

In the morning say, "whatever";
in the evening say, "enough."

"Whatever" is a modern way of saying,
"Thy will be done."

Give it away to keep it.

Don't get attached to either income
or outcome.

I have held many things in my hands, and I
have lost them all; but whatever I have placed
in God's hands, that I still possess.

—Martin Luther

The power of surrender cannot be taught,
it can only be experienced.

My need to live without alcohol does not
mean that my loved one is wrong
to live with it.

Most people change not because they see the
light, but because they feel the heat.

We don't see the world as it is.
We see the world as we are.

The toughest lesson to learn is probably the one you thought you already learned.

God has a great plan for you if you will just get out of the way.

We can't fly till we let go of the dirt.

Men may rise on stepping stones of their dead selves to higher things.

—Alfred, Lord Tennyson

While we point a finger at others, God is pointing three fingers back at us.

God helps those who don't try to take over His work.

You get to the point where your demons,
which are terrifying, get smaller and smaller,
and you get bigger and bigger.

—August Wilson

You grow up the day you have the first
real laugh—at yourself.

—Ethel Barrymore

The elevator to recovery is broken . . .
you'll have to use the Steps.

Step 1 . . . I can't.
Step 2 . . . He can.
Step 3 . . . So I'll let Him.

We are a group of winners
living through losing situations.

Humility just means you're teachable.

The smaller I am, the bigger He is.

Grace comes in two forms: getting what you want and getting what you don't want.

Humility is to fall on fertile ground.
—Greek proverb

I came for the doughnuts,
but now I come for the Steps.

We learn that Steps 1, 2, and 3 tell us, "Give up."
Steps 4, 5, and 6 tell us, "Clean up."
Steps 7, 8, and 9 tell us, "Make up."
And Steps 10, 11, and 12 tell us, "Grow up."

We discover we do receive guidance for our lives to the extent that we stop making demands upon God to give it to us on order and on our terms.

—*Twelve Steps and Twelve Traditions*

FAITH:
Fantastic Adventure In Trusting Him.

Be willing to be willing.

Trace it, face it, and erase it.

When you're in God's army, you never know
where you'll be stationed.

When I have surrendered to God's perfect
will, I will have His perfect peace.

I have outgrown the need to suffer.

Giving and Receiving

When everything else fails, try gratitude.

If you don't know how to pray,
ask God to help you.

If you don't have a God, use my God.
He's big enough for both of us.

In Al-Anon we love you
until you love yourself.

I had a hole in myself so big
that only a group this big can fill it.

The first time I ever heard the Twelve Steps
read at a meeting, I became very still.
I was not breathing, just listening with my
whole being. I knew deep within me that
I was home.

Sometimes I go about pitying myself
and all the while I am being carried across the sky
by beautiful clouds.

—Ojibway Indian saying

Have a Gratitude Attitude.

Share your experience, joy, and hope.

Love builds highways out of dead ends.

—Louis Gittner

God loves you as you are, but too much
to leave you as you are.

Think of yourself as a gift.
If you are accepted, fine;
if not, fine.

—Terry Lynn Taylor

A giver is only a channel for God's gifts.
One cannot hoard or withhold them
without blocking the channel.

Doubt closes the door to miracles.

To see miracles, let go of expectation.

Coincidence is God's way
of remaining anonymous.

Angels are manifested into being by the
human need to see them.

If you have gratitude, you have happiness.
—Terry Lynn Taylor

If you're not lucky enough to have an alcoholic
in your life, go out and borrow one.

I have learned silence from the talkative,
tolerance from the intolerant,
and kindness from the unkind.
I should not be ungrateful to those teachers.

—Kahlil Gibran

Be grateful when thorns have roses.

Flowers are put on earth to remind you to say
"Thanks."

If the only prayer you said in your whole life
was "Thank you" that would suffice.

—Meister Eckhart

Meditation is that out-of-focus state between
thoughts where one finds ultimate clarity.

Prayer is speaking to God;
meditation is listening to God.

Not repeating my old behaviors
is making amends to me.

Thank you for all the good I did today and
all the good I did by not doing.

Whatever I need to know is revealed to me,
and whatever I need comes in divine
right order.

Thank your parents for giving birth to you—
everything else is by divine arrangement.

Laughter is the language of angels.

Flowers always leave a fragrance in the hand
that bestows them.

In the midst of winter, I finally learned that there was in me an invincible summer.

—Albert Camus

Gifts come when we learn to see beauty in all persons, especially in those we despise.

I don't have to like everyone to love them.

Al-Anon is a healthy womb environment.

When you touch a fellow human being with
love, you are doing God's work.

—Emmanuel

All I have to offer anyone is my own
experience of the truth.

—*Courage to Change*

Call me after you call someone even
newer than you.

—Al-Anon sponsor

As you focus on what is good about people,
you enable them to achieve it.

—Sanaya Roman

We are best able to help others when we ourselves have learned the way to achieve serenity.

A successful man was asked, "What has helped you over the great obstacles of life?" "The other obstacles," he replied.

Happiness is an inside job.

I have a lot better problems today than I've ever had.

Rejoice in the success of others.

We are members of one another.

—Romans 12:5

There, but for the grace of God go I.

God alone knows the secret plan of the things
he will do for the world using my hand.

—Toyohiko Kagawa

When something is taken from my life, it
means God has something better for me.

Earth laughs in flowers.

—Ralph Waldo Emerson

We don't always get what we want,
but we get what we need.

Thankful means you're glad it happened.
Grateful means you want to do something
in return.

Beauty is in the eye of the beholder—me!

Wisdom

God, grant me the serenity to
accept the things I cannot change,
the courage to change the things I can,
and the wisdom to know the difference.

Living one day at a time,
enjoying one moment at a time,
accepting hardship as the pathway to peace.
Trusting that he would make all things right
if I surrender to his will.

—Reinhold Niebuhr

Example is not the main thing in influencing
others. It is the only thing.

—Albert Schweitzer

You learn to speak by speaking, to study
by studying, to run by running, to work by
working, and just so you learn to love
God and man by loving.

—Francis de Sales

Don't lock yourself in an elevator,
leaving others to push the buttons.

There is no free lunch.
There are, however, better places to eat.

It's better to be silent and thought a fool than
to open your mouth and remove all doubt.

—Will Rogers

Humility isn't thinking less of one's self;
it's thinking of one's self less.

The greatest discovery of my generation is
that a human being can alter his life
by altering his attitudes.

—William James

The principle that keeps us in perpetual
ignorance is contempt prior to investigation.

Where is there dignity unless there is honesty.

—Marcus Tullius Cicero

The toughest year of marriage is usually
the one you're in.

Argue for your limitations,
and sure enough they're yours.

—Richard Bach

The highest form of wisdom is kindness.
—The Talmud

Knowing others is wisdom,
knowing oneself is enlightenment.

God help me be the person my dog thinks I am.

Love doesn't make the world go around,
but it makes the ride worthwhile.

Don't mistake devices for principles.

When the student is ready,
the teacher will appear.

We teach what we most need to learn.

There is guidance for each of us, and by lowly
listening we shall hear the right word.

—Ralph Waldo Emerson

By listening to more than mere words, I can learn much more than mere words can teach.

Besides the noble art of getting things done, there is the noble art of leaving things undone. The wisdom of life consists in the elimination of nonessentials.

—Lin Yü-tang

It is the privilege of wisdom to listen.

—Oliver Wendell Holmes

It is not that seeing is believing,
but believing is seeing.

The thing always happens that you really
believe in; and the belief in a thing
makes it happen.

—Frank Lloyd Wright

Use your intelligence to find reasons to
support your intuition.

If alcohol or drugs are the answer to your problem, what the hell is the question?

What difference does it make if you've got God on the line if you're beating yourself to death with the receiver.

HOW we recover:
Honesty, **O**pen-mindedness, **W**illingness.

Serenity is not freedom from the storm,
but Peace amid the storm.

Don't mistake comfort for freedom.

Laughter is a tranquilizer with no side effects.

If we do not change our direction, we are
likely to end up where we are headed.

—Chinese proverb

The first place I need to go for help
is to my Higher Power.

We each get here right on time.

When I pedal and let God steer,
we really go places.
When I steer, I just go in circles.

Resentment is as poisonous to me as any drug.

My inner child is a juvenile delinquent.

When old behavior is uncomfortable, it is a good sign that it's time for a change.

Think our way into right acting.
Act our way into right thinking.

God, give me peace in my heart, serenity in my soul, and laughter on my face.

The best way I've found to invite serenity is to recognize that the world is in good hands.

—Courage to Change

The meaning of prayer is that we get hold of God, not the answer.

I need to give up being my invention
so I can be God's creation.

If you understand, things are just as they are;
if you do not understand, things are
just as they are.

—Zen proverb

All you have to do is love God, love other
people, and love yourself; the rest of it is gravy.

God is seldom early, but He's never late.

God grant me the serenity to accept
the people I cannot change,
the courage to change the person I can,
and the wisdom to know it's me.

Dear Reader,

Please write the author with a favorite saying or higher power experience for a book in progress. Stories should be 500 words or less. Your written *share* will be treated with the same respect and anonymity as if given at a meeting. Thank you for offering your higher power experience of strength and hope to others.

Please include a self-addressed envelope.

Write to:
Barbara F.
1409 Fifth Street
Suite D
Berkeley, CA 94709

Selected Bibliography

Al-Anon Family Group Headquarters, Inc. *Al-Anon's Twelve Steps and Twelve Traditions*. New York: Al-Anon Family Group, 1993.

———. *Courage to Change*. New York: Al-Anon Family Group, 1992.

———. *The Dilemma of the Alcoholic Marriage*. New York: Al-Anon Family Group, 1991.

———. *From Survival to Recovery*. New York: Al-Anon Family Group, 1994.

———. *In All Our Affairs*. New York: Al-Anon Family Group, 1990.

———. *One Day at a Time in Al-Anon*. New York: Al-Anon Family Group, 1989.

Alcoholics Anonymous World Services, Inc. *Alcoholics Anonymous.* New York: Alcoholics Anonymous World Services, 1976.

_____. *Came to Believe.* New York: Alcoholics Anonymous World Services, 1986.

_____. *Twelve Steps and Twelve Traditions.* New York: Alcoholics Anonymous World Services, 1953.

Estés, Clarissa Pinkola. *Women Who Run with the Wolves.* New York: Ballantine Books, 1992.

Fishel, Ruth. *Time for Joy.* Deerfield Beach, Fla.: Health Communications, Inc., 1988.

Lerner, Harriet Goldhor. *The Dance of Anger.* New York: Harper and Row, 1985.

Meera, Mother. *Answers.* London: Rider, 1991.

Merton, Thomas. *The Way of Chuang Tzu.* Boston: Shambhala, 1992.

Roman, Sanaya. *Personal Power Through Awareness.* Edited by Elaine Ratner. Tiburon, Calif.: H. J. Kramer, Inc., 1986.

Tannen, Deborah. *That's Not What I Meant.* New York: Ballantine Books, 1987.

Taylor, Terry Lynn. *Creating with the Angels*. Tiburon, Calif.: H. J. Kramer, Inc., 1993.

Tsai, Chi Chung. *Zen Speaks*. New York: Anchor Books, Doubleday, 1994.

Other titles that will interest you . . .

My Mind Is Out to Get Me
Humor and Wisdom in Recovery
compiled by Dr. Ron B.
Five hundred inspirational quotes that highlight the wonderful oral tradition, wisdom, and humor found in sobriety. This rich resource of memorable adages gathered from real people working the Twelve Steps has helped millions in their own recovery. 168 pp.
Order No. 1319

For price and order information, or a free catalog, please call our Telephone Representatives.

HAZELDEN

1-800-328-0098
(Toll Free., U.S., Canada
and the Virgin Islands)

1-651-213-4000
(Outside the U.S. and Canada)

1-651-213-4590
(24-Hour FAX)

Pleasant Valley Road • Box 176 • Center City, MN 55012-0176
www.hazelden.org